old state road

two stories of a place that sustained us

Poems by Jason Gerrish
Photographs by Brad Daulton

UnCollected Press

old state road.
Copyright©2021 by Jason Gerrish and Brad Daulton.

Cover: *devil and his banjo #6, tintype* by Brad Daulton.

Grateful acknowledgement is made to Henry Stanton and to The Raw Art Review, where some of these poems and photographs first appeared.

Brad and Jason would also like to thank Amy, Kristin, and Kay Daulton, without whom none of this book would be possible.

ISBN: 978-1-7360098-5-7

to June Dryden

Table of Contents

the lane, late afternoon, tintype 1

polarity 2

first dusting, tintype 3

the trailer: an introduction 4

the farm on Old State Road, tintype 11

walking papers 12

axe in post, tintype 14

What's bad is factory work 15

snow in the field, tintype 18

woodland snow, tintype 19

crow 20

gypsy horse skull and rosary, ambrotype 22

you know, a loneliness 23

branches and canes, tintype 28

the knotted flesh 29

smokehouse and shed, tintype 30

how it happened 31

barn, foundation, skull, tintype 33

bastard outside 34

this old woman I like 36

around a nightly fire, ambrotype 38

flying squirrel 39

plow, tintype 40

abandoned 41

barn in summer, tintype	42
lemon	43
barn near dark, ambrotype	45
What's good is being the dishwasher	46
early evening walk, ambrotype	49
you, your cat, and I	50
the lane, ambrotype	52
Bealya	53
smokehouse, ambrotype	55
overdose	56
two trees, tintype	57
she was… she was… she was…	58
woven trees, tintype	60
a really bad night	61
gourd, tintype	65
Aideen	66
flowers, tintype	68
ode to apocalypse	69
trunk and vine, tintype	70
the lone oak	71
angst	73
devil and his banjo, tintype	80
cello suite	81
skulls and bones, tintype	84
dead poem #9	85
the musician's fate, tintype	87

old state road

the lane, late afternoon, tintype

polarity

waking,   late
feeling the need for
yet another baptism.

starting a shower,   the jet
blasting the vinyl curtain
muting the noise in my head.

stripping,   before
the fogging mirror,
and stepping into the tub,

the rushing torrent,
recharging my
dulled perception.

glancing down and catching
a glimpse of something moving,
in the slow draining water, at my feet.

a spider,

trapped in a tiny whirlpool,
dragging her down the drain.

fate of spiders.

first dusting, tintype

the trailer: an introduction

Early winter, afternoon,
I followed Brad, out 52
anxious, and yet,
it was a quiet drive,
except for the muffled
roaming sounds
of my gray Monte Carlo.

More than once,
I had been with Brad
to his family farm,
but I still could not find
the place, on my own.

He took me east along the river,
about an hour from Cincinnati.
Just before the Maysville Bridge,
we turned left on 41.
I lit a smoke, and took
notice of the way.

There were many common houses,
as we were still close to town,
but after a sideroad
called Fishing Gut,
the road became a low passage
through the rolling hills, thick
with bare, winter trees,
here and there, a drive
and a doublewide.

Then a creek appeared on the left,
and the road seemed to follow it,

passed a gothic farmhouse
and a one-room shack
with a rusted roof.

Brad turned right on Buttermilk,
and we immediately began to climb
to the high ground
and Old State Road,
where it became lighter
and much of the land
along the crest was cleared.

I was drawn to a tobacco basket
propped up against a wall,
by a rocking chair,
on a modest, white porch.

There were outbuildings
and more house trailers,
but I also saw dark,
grizzly barns
and lonesome,
stark,
harvested fields.

Near Ginger Ridge,
Brad slowed down
and threw on
his left turn signal;
it was the first time
I laid eyes on the trailer;
I had not paid it
any mind,
the times I'd been before.

It was a short distance from the farm
and on the opposite side the street.
Right of the trailer
was a shade tree
and enough gravel pad
to park two cars.

We got out, stretched,
and I looked around.

The trailer was a Fleetwood,
about fifty feet long,
flat white, sun faded,
with dull green trim.
Behind it was a yard
of tawny, dormant grass
that sloped abruptly
to a wooded hollow.

Two steps took us up
to a square,
red-brown deck,
and Brad unlocked the door.

We stood on ragged
seafoam green shag,
in a neat, open area,
between the kitchen
and the living room.

Medium brown, paneled walls
made the space feel
dull
and narrow.

A large mirror hung
over a dark green couch,
a plain coffee table,
and two chairs,
old burgundy and olive green,
with a lamp on
an octagon
end table,
between.

I caught a faint whiff
of propane from the pilot,
on the glossy, avocado
kitchen stove.

"This is it," said Brad.
I could see his breath, as
he adjusted the thermostat.

He gave me a quick tour:
kitchen
living room
hall
small bedroom
bathroom
small bedroom.

"Do you want to bring
anything in,
from your car?"
he asked.

"Nah," I said,
 I'll get it tomorrow."

"Cool. Let's walk next door
and say hi to grandmother,
then I'll take you into town,
and we'll get some beer."

His grandmother's name was June.
I had met her before,
first on thanksgiving, in'91,
but this was different,
I was 27, and moving in,
just down and across the street.

She came to the storm door
grinning, shyly,
with few teeth.

June was little, an old farmgirl
with short and wavy, white hair.

She wore thick eyeglasses,
and each time she blinked,
her blue eyes reemerged,
appearing too large for her face.

June was grand.
June was sincere.

"Ohh… Hi… Are you moving in
to the trailer, now?" she said.

"Hi, Grandma."

"Yes," I said.

"Are you boys hungry? I have
some beans and corn bread?"

"No, were fine," said Brad.

"You think you'll like living
out here?" she asked me.

"I do."

"Good. You come over
whenever you like.
I like company."

We drove down Roush Hill
into Manchester,
bought beer and cigarettes
at a liquor store,
made a loop, passed a grocery,
so that I knew where it was,
and then back up to Old State
and the trailer.

We drank.

"So,
do you think you can teach
yourself to write out here?"
asked Brad.

"We'll see.
That's the plan."

"You need to write like a boxer.

A boxer doesn't enter the ring
looking for a knockout.
When the bell rings,
a boxer comes forward
and goes to work on you."

We talked all-night.

In the morning,
Brad drove back to the city
and I started to settle in.

the farm on Old State Road, tintype

walking papers

there was a knock at the door
I got up from my writing to answer it
in came the caravan of loneliness
now they won't leave
I throw beer cans at them and
they only look at me with sad eyes.

I don't have the energy
to throw them out yet,
but I will
there is only so much a man can take
before he must expose the myth
about safety in numbers.

I throw a chair up in the air
"Get out! We are all lost!
Nothing ever works out the way we plan.
Now GO!
Get yourselves a good meal
and part company."

The last one out the door
pours me whiskey to the brim
it is, in a way,
hard to see them go.
yes,
it is sad.

I can hear my mother screaming
and contesting with my father;
was he lying in their bed
with a rifle pointed on her,
when, at nine years old,

I walked in and froze?

I think about Joanna,
the night we first kissed;
how it was all meant to happen.
How there was nothing between us
in that moment, when
mortal love bursts?

axe in post, tintype

What's bad is factory work

What's bad is 2nd shift
and seven 10s, for a month straight.
What's bad is the drudging spirit of the place;
the obscene hum of 300 people
standing in front of sewing machines.

What's good is thinking about someplace else.

What's good is grasping at curtains.
What's good is a blizzard.
What's good is the sheriff,
closing all the roads.

What's good is new paper
new ribbon and knowing that
no one will be stopping by.

I work at the Miss-Pu-Pee-She plant
across the river in Kentucky.
Ten hours a day, seven days a week,
they train me to sew leather seats.
They must plan on selling lots of cars.

I was running out of money
and I couldn't write shit
all the crap that was in me
that I thought I could unload with ease
just wouldn't come out;
all I did was drink,
smoke,
eat,
until my stockpile
was nearly exhausted.

So I took the job.

I've been smart though
with my dirty green sewing money
I've been paying my bills forward, and
I did my research and determined
the cheapest beer and cigarettes
I can stand.

I'll fill the freezer with lunch meat and bread
and rib eyes (when they go on sale).

What's bad is a 30 pack of Keystone.
What's bad is a carton of Dorals.

What's confusing is factory girls.
The tender one training me to sew
caught me looking at her ass,
round and grown
like a pumpkin.

"What are you doing, Hal?
Do you think you can learn to sew?"

She has soft eyes,
pale skin, and high,
rose-pink cheeks.

"It ain't that bad," she says,
"There's a lot of couples that work here,
and they'll raise a family with this job."

I may have asked
if she ever read poetry.

What's good is an apparatus
to get things moving.

What's good is 8 cases of Milwaukee's Best Light
all stacked in the closet, because
you can't fit any more in the fridge.

snow in the field, tintype

woodland snow, tintype

crow

I was not preoccupied that morning;
I was just fixing a cup of coffee.
Then, through a gap in the kitchen curtain,
I caught sight of June, outside in the cold,
hasting and doddering up Old State Road,
with her spectacles and large troubled eyes;
and when I saw that she was entering my yard,
I hurried too and unbolted the door.
"Hal, your mother's been trying to reach you,"
June said, "your grandmother has passed away."

Nobody had my new phone number yet.
I tried calling mom, but the line was busy;
and I could not relax in your absence.
It didn't feel like you were really gone,
though I worried where it was that you went.
I troubled myself to remember,
but I couldn't settle on your dark eyes,
and I couldn't picture your fixed, dark hair,
just that it was always fixed, always black,
even at sixty-years, black…black as jet.

I did remember a certain morning
waking rested in your quiet home.
I was maybe seven, or eight, or nine.
We met one another in the kitchen.
You squeezed my cheeks and said, "cabecinha",
made me coffee with milk and with sugar,
and told me stories, of when you were young.
Hanging on to your every word,
I only sipped on my coffee slowly,
so, I didn't empty my cup too soon.

"Your mother, paciencia," you began,
"I used to wait for her to come home from school;
in those days, children walked to and from school,
and I use to wait outside in the yard,
everyday. Well, one day she didn't come home.
I waited and waited, but she didn't come.
I was so worried, I started to walk
toward the school, to find out where she was.
As soon as I left our driveway, I looked
and what do I see coming down our road?

This pathetic little thing, your mother,
with a great black crow standing on her head.
Oh my god, she was crying and crying;
she was barely moving, she was so afraid,
and that dreadful bird would not fly away.
It dug a talon in your mother's brow,
and that awful thing would not let go.
It left a scar; it's still there, you'll see it;
ask her about the big black crow that came
to land on her head... Would you like more coffee?"

cabecinha - my grandmother pronounced: cub-seen-ya.
for her it was a term of endearment, meaning "you have a cute little head, but you know nothing."

paciencia – my grandmother pronounced: pa-see-an-sah
she regularly used this word to invoke a saint or deity to give her patience.

gypsy horse skull and rosary, ambrotype

you know, a loneliness

Her husband was in the Navy.
She missed him,
but missing him
didn't do her any good.
We got together a couple times,
and she made me feel
like the only person
in the room.

"Being married is fine," she said,
"I'm happy to belong to Joe,
and I get the best of his love.
I worry about him, but I know
he's taking care of himself.
Anyway, somebody's
got to be
getting fucked."

When we finished, she said,
"You know,
all you men are about an inch too short."

"Hey," I said,
"you didn't like it?"

"You couldn't tell?" she answered,
"If I don't like it,
I'll let you know."

I got off the bed and went to the front window.
Dull khaki people walked by the open curtains.
"You know, they can see in here plain as day," she said.

I lit a cigarette and spread my stance,
"Why should I care? We're all an inch too short.
Let them get a good look and see for themselves."

"I was just teasing," she said,
"You're actually very well endowed."

"Really?"

"No,
but get out of the window.
Let's get dressed and go to the bar."

There was a good crowd at the 500 Club.
We drank vodka, soda and watched them.

"Look at that one," she said, and pointed
at a tall blonde guy, in a striped shirt.
He was standing over a brunette at the bar.
She wore a low-cut, black dress,
and yielded a dry smile.
The striped shirt was talking her ears off.
"Can't he see she's really not interested?"

"Poor thing," I said,
"but Christ, what an ego,
I wonder how long he can keep it up?"

"Oh, god, she's having a terrible night.
We should rescue her."

"How? Should I find her a plunger?"

Four hours into the drink
she mentioned Joe
had a scheduled port visit
and would probably call.

She ordered another vodka,
but I asked the bartender
for a water.

"Water?
You can't hang?" she asked.

"Just my way of making it last."

"It isn't going to last," she said.

"What? You're not having a good time?"

"I'm having the time of my life."
She downed her drink and walked outside,
leaving me at the bar.

I felt dumb sitting there.
I didn't wait long,
finished my water,
and followed her.

She wobbled on the edge of the sidewalk
with a cigarette between her lips,
fumbling through her purse.
I handed her my lighter.

I saw it, then.

I leaned in
to touch my lips
to a salty tear,
holding to her cheek.

"Stop it," she said,
and turned
back inward.

"Let me walk you home.
Let me hold you a little."

She became discrete.

The moths rattled
in the dead light
and flew into one another.

"You can take me home," she said,
but you need to leave in the morning,
and we need to take a break,
you know?"

I lay awake
while she slept,
warm flesh bound
by warm flesh
in her drafty room
quiet, but for
a faucet dripping
and the thud
of her cat leaping,
from counter

to floor.

Birds called
in the courtyard, waiting
for the sun to burn a hole
through the time of our life.

branches and canes, tintype

the knotted flesh

it was early morning
her place,
and I felt bad
being there.

I thought
it would be better
at my place,
but I was wrong.

I had left my
kitchen window
propped open
and flies buzzed
my coffee,
face and
ashtray.

I closed the window

and must, now, endure:

the knotted flesh,

the frantic droning
that haunts the gap
between glass
and final curtain.

smokehouse and shed, tintype

how it happened

"For Christ's sake, you don't want to live with them, do you?"
"No," I said, receiving the bag
from Lawson's Hardware.
"Well, it's not going to make you a goddamn Nazi.
Just remember… the sooner the better."

The first one went in the middle of the night.
It looked swift, sudden, like a painless sleep.
There was more blood with the second,
sticking to the hair near the wound,
the white hair about the belly.

They had done nothing wrong for months, but I began
to find little black rice shit everywhere, and
they gnawed at the page edges
of Whitman and Frost, and made
a nest of my down sleeping bag.

Several went right in line then.
There was barely ten minutes between them.
One after the other, they went right in,
but the worst came when I found
the trap does not always finish them.

The steel striker springs at 30 meters per second.
So loaded, it closes on the neck or the skull,
but the brain may fizzle out slowly,
scrambled with pain signals,
and they cry, as if for mercy.

I took one in such condition outdoors;
saw his plump red heart swell within his chest,
his gut heaved, for the lungs to surge,

desperate,
to get at the air.

I crushed him beneath my foot, to
"put him down quick" as they say, but
I couldn't stand for it. I had to sit,
and take whiskey and cigarettes
to clean the blood from my sole.

Another had just a small wound, top his head
(though I suppose it may have been enough).
I took him behind the trailer,
to the edge of the woods
and let him down.

He shook, but had strength in him still to crawl
beneath a drift of fallen leaves.
Sooner or later,
this is how it happened.
I dug the hole.

barn, foundation, skull, tintype

bastard outside

he is branded
stranded on corners
sitting on discarded newsprint
a crazed madman
he mutters ought
and obsesses over fragments.

the corners of his eyes and mouth
caked with dry discharge
he'll keep rancid
layered in remnants and an overcoat
coughing up phlegm
and smoking butts off the sidewalk.

how they are made that way
we'll never know
the division is cut
so that most days
we will not even notice
they are being
anything but crazed madmen
hanging in the balance
bastards know the worth of $5
better than we
today and tomorrow
to get it
for their daily bread
a cup of coffee
or a bottle of rotgut.

I look too
and wish not to see,
not today,

I know how to get myself a drink
or two
and that's all.

this old woman I like

This old woman,
this horde of flesh wrapped in a tablecloth,
approaches the front desk doggedly,
longing to pass on some bit of information
that she has readied on the tip of her tongue.

Her eyes are arrows, but her arms
are like the torn retreads I dodge,
abandoned along the edge of the freeway,
and her lips are thin and flat,
behind a spread of rouge.

She shoves a wastebasket in my face.
"The god damn maid didn't take out my trash
or leave me any clean towels."
"That bitch," I mutter, a little too loudly,
because I too have been glossed over.

I walk to the back,
dump her trash,
and get two clean towels.
"If there's anything else," I tell her,
"just let me know."

"There ain't," she says,
and exiting the lobby,
she topples a floor lamp with her cane,
and she calls a wet, young blond in a bikini
a "stupid whore".

"What's her problem?" asks the wet bikini.
"She's just old," I say, "and her clothes don't fit her."
Nearing her room, at the end of the hall,
unadorned, the Old Woman succeeds,
"Fuck you, too."

around a nightly fire, ambrotype

flying squirrel

talking with Brad in the field
reading Ginsburg by the fire
countryside was good for drinking
though we hoped by morning's hour
something more would be revealed.

in vain we howled for beauty
as cold and dark were like a cloak
'til we were forced to gather more kindling
and that tiny, woodland pixie flew
over the lane and out of view.

plow, tintype

abandoned

When you are bent, I will not bloom,
and poesy becomes a tomb.
The evidence I disappoint you,
I'm so inconsistent.

You do nothing, save get some sleep.
I lie flat at the window and while.
It's a shame to keep chaste in this myth,
to remain unsatisfied.

Behind each line, an ardent moment,
your tongue, your pen feigned to eulogize.
I will be fine if you're ready to leave me;
I'll sustain this cold cant not versified,

but when every minute haunts you,
come to find me drifting loosely,
distant and incomplete. Go Now!
Catch the pox with the wild girls.

barn in summer, tintype

lemon

I called you on the phone, but you were busy
you said the phrase "having the time of your life".

I hung up on you because I am
a "self-centered, arrogant, son of a bitch".

A stopped sink, clogged with lemon peels;
I founder and lurk about the foul, seafoam carpet.

My feet stink, and I have no clean socks,
lying beside my fetid and perverted subjects:

an ornery band of crushed cigarette butts,
rallied about a toppled ashtray.

We jeer at the coffee table of Milwaukee's,
liking to a beer-soaked, burlesque stage.

I've been trickling out fragmented letters
for days now and tossing them to the floor.

For weeks, I've held up, but now,
the tide recedes; the truth litters the shore;

all my life, wasted on this thing that I am,
wasted on the thing I am not.

Let my words be swift like the swallow's shadow:
rising from barn walls, twisting in the sun,

snaking in and out of the gloom.
Let there be no rest, no end to this illusion.

I am here, Muse! Sitting in the olive armchair,
fingertips over the keys. Why will Nothing come?

Am I odious and sickening? Did you ever see
anything? Anything, but the worst of me?

Rising, and nearly losing my balance,
I yank the phone out of the wall!

I AM the King! of the wet roll of toilet paper
which I accidentally dropped into the commode,

the roll I plucked out, that oozed with my retrieval,
all over the yellowing, dandelion linoleum.

I AM the King! of these impish fellows,
these nasty butts and ashes and these lewd whiskey bottles.

Stumbling to the mirror, with the alarm in my head,
I strip the afghan from the couch and decorate my shoulders.

I AM THE KING! of empty cans and clogged disposals,
the king of murky dishwater and vulgar magazines.

I AM the King, of dirty socks
here and there, and behind the sofa,

and of the words on the page, scattered about the floor;
and it is I in these words that will be lost someday, finally.

This is a place for me, of lemon peels and dirty socks.
It has chosen me, like mortality.

My bird thrashes and rattles, nailed to rough oak planks,
painted red and beaten by the wind.

barn near dark, ambrotype

What's good is being the dishwasher

What's good are the waitresses
and all the half-full bottles of wine
they bring with the mucked-up plates.
I pour them in coffee mugs,
so no one can see what I'm drinking.

What's bad is musculum contagiosum.
What's bad is wanting someone
more than they want you.

What's good is her dark eyes.
What's good is her bare neck and shoulders
in the low-cut, blue summer dress.

I once lived with a woman in Oakland
she came home each night and told me about her day
I could listen to her every word
every word was unpleasant and promising.
Her feet stunk from standing in worn shoes for hours
I would rub mint lotion on her soles
about her toes
and I would listen.
She insisted we make love every night
and in the morning, we would look on the other
and be cute in her shower
lathering one another up
until it was time to get dressed
and start it all over.
I haven't seen that woman in years
I don't even have a photo of her now.

What's bad is drinking heavy at a blackjack table.
What's bad is doubling down on a hard 12

What's worse is splitting 10s.

What's good is the river
What's good is a stiff drink
on the bare upper deck of a casino boat,
rolling down the Mississippi at 1am, alone.

What's bad is owing money to people you care about.
What's bad is borrowing money you don't want to earn.
What's worse is seeing people you borrowed from,
out at a bar.

I spent a night in jail in Kentucky
there was not an innocent man in the cell.
The guards wouldn't give me my cigarettes.
A man inside for not paying child support
spotted me several smokes.
The mother of a good friend
drove 50 miles to pay my bail.

What's bad is young men with too much to say.
What's profound is old men who say nothing.

What's good is a day
that doesn't demand you get dressed.
What's bad is socks with holes.
What's good is sadness
when you know it is all
you are ever going to find.

My father lives
somewhere in Rhode Island
I haven't heard from him in years
I show him alone in a room

there are no pictures on the wall
no telephone
only a clock and an ashtray
and a window that is cold.

What's bad is wondering how her eyes finally saw you.
What's bad is rolling your car off Ginger Ridge.
What's bad is she won't take your calls.
What's bad is watching her walk.

What's awkward is tomorrow.
What's strange is praying at last.

What's good is bourbon
What's good is single malt whiskey.

What's good is pretending
that she hasn't changed.

early evening walk, ambrotype

you, your cat, and I

Between seven and eight in the evening,
a brilliant blue, an aura, almost neon,
hung briefly, like a ghost, over Oakland,
and drew me out of George Kaye's Bar.

By then I'd have more than a few drinks in;
I'd reminisce how our old love walked down on
Broadway, through the intersection,
and west on 41st.

We'd be returning home with coffee from
a café around the corner. I'd hear
you singing and I'd hear our laughter
as we went strolling in a dream.

A dream within a dream! I'd allow it
to lure me on across the street,
but always some crack in the sidewalk
reminded me, I was alone.

The last time I walked down 41st Street,
I had been unable to sleep for days;
midnight and moonless, I hesitated,
till I saw the streetlight outside your home.

It was there your cat found me and sitting
down on the curb we looked on the other
carefully and remembered when
I understood my being there was wrong.

Though I felt I was only dreaming,
I feared your cat might try to follow me,
'til the anxious whisper of another
lone apparition drew him away.

He danced with a moth, to dusty wings were lost,
withdrawn all at once into staid, dark night;
then, turned down your path and glided up
the steps, into the light about your door.

the lane, ambrotype

Bealya

We were drinking in the sub galley.
She was a tall red head with freckles everywhere.
She told me her name, but it wasn't important;
I had no intentions.

She looked like a Bealya.
I did see her freckles,
clear as the spots
on a brown trout pear.

I spent my last few dollars buying us a draft each,
and if Bealya was broke, I would not have hung on.
The napkins stuck
to our glasses of cold beer.

When her money was nearly gone,
we walked toward her place on Jefferson,
but stopped along the way,
and Bealya asked what I wanted to drink.

A pint of Old Crow left change for a scratch off,
which I insisted she buy.
The ticket was good for $10, that
Bealya spent, on a bottle of wine.

Her apartment was on the third floor
of a tall narrow home.
The heat collected there,
and a weary fan blew the heat around.

Natural light whispered
through dull, blue shears,
and low angular ceilings

forced Bealya and I together.

We set the fan directly on us
and stripped to our underwear,
then Bealya
put on a thin robe.

She fixed my whiskey for me,
with ice and with water,
rinsed a wine glass for herself,
and we sat.

She said that growing up,
she hated her complexion,
and it wasn't until her late twenties
that she got used to it.

Notes of violet spread
from Bealya's glass around the room,
and from her mouth
to my thoughts.

The day emptied, and we fell
together on the couch;
I held Bealya
and I listened to her breathe.

I studied her freckles
delicate and random
like downy seeds of dandelion
in flight, when a field is mowed in spring.

smokehouse, ambrotype

overdose

a pale, shrouded earth,
i failed to emerge,
from a weak lawn chair,
on crooked ground.

the crows spoke harshly
from a nearby tree.
the neighbors watched me
sitting alone.

the air i breathed
was resolved and dry;
it would not gather
or make a sound.

i had money for beer,
but the stores at last closed.

two trees, tintype

she was… she was… she was…

and what else is now for,
but desperate barrooms,
full of prayer and whisky,
beer lights, neon,
and lonely dollar bills?

now I restrain
the instinct to call,
just to hear
your soft voice.
I shroud the urge;
I bury it in my gut,
as if it were not real.

now is cold and deadly.
now is for telling lies.

she was… she was… she was…

I strain through the silence
and squander my withholdings,
relating them to any
benevolent ear.

When I stumble to my car,
after last call,
I fumble with the keys,
and finish the night
reaching and curling about
the front seat, beneath
a peacoat, drifting,

like a dinghy,
rocking
through rough water.

tomorrow, the sun rises
but I will lay low
wanting for the expression in your eyes,
to know we are more than passing frames.

woven trees, tintype

a really bad night

Someone phoned;
it woke me.

Who would be calling
at 3 a.m.?

What could be so
important?

I pulled the afghan
from back the couch

and covered,
best I could.

The ringer went silent,
then, began again.

What did they want?
I advanced my trunk,

beyond sofa's edge,
legs still

riding the cushions.
Over sea foam

carpet, I stretched,
snagged the receiver

and answered,
"Hello!"

"Hello," said a voice.
It was June.

"What are you doing?" she said,
like a jarred carriage,

"Was you
asleep?"

I pictured her old
inquisitive face,

her blue eyes
and large glasses.

"No," I said, "I
was just lying down."

Feeling dumb
for getting riled,

I recoiled,
beneath the afghan.

"Boy, it's a bad
storm, isn't it?"

"Is it?"
I said.

"Yeah. Mmm Hmm.
It's a bad storm."

Sleep drunk, I listened
and noticed it then.

I drew myself up
and lit a cigarette.

The rain was really coming
down hard, and thunder.

"Wow,"
I said.

"Mmm Hmm.
It's a real bad storm.

I'm scared.
Are you scared?"

We are all, too much
of the time, anxious.

"It is pretty
scary," I said.

"I know," said June,
"Do you

want to come over?
Play some cards?"

I was sure to get doused
to play gin, in dank clothes.

"Do you have
coffee?" I asked.

"I can make some
coffee."

"Turn the back light on for me.
I'll get dressed and be over."

"Oh, yeah,
I'll put the light on for you.

Okay then.
Bye."

gourd, tintype

Aideen

Once again, the wind blows through the trees
and carries the leaves to the ground.
Bound to this land, and bound to my shame,
it's your name I hear echo through these hills.

Caught you out drinking with that Caudill boy,
Oh my Aideen, where are you now.
Think about it, and my blood still boils,
Oh my Aideen, where are you now.

Sometimes I know that it looks awful strange,
I'm roaming the holler below;
and on clear days, I climb to the balds above,
but then they're just places we use to go.

Forty hours and a beat-up car,
Oh my Aideen, where are you now.
The melody is in a mason jar,
Oh my Aideen, where are you now.

A floor that needs sweeping, no food upon the shelf,
a table that needs wiped down,
shards of broken glass, beside old photographs,
and a ring near a watch that needs wound,

I think about you, and my hands won't rest,
Oh my Aideen, where are you now.
Words are hollow, empty in my chest,
Oh my Aideen, where are you now.

A tight fitted bed gathers dust in a room,
abandoned at the end of the hall;
dust on the windows, dust on old blooms,
inside and outside these walls.

I should get out, but it won't happen soon,
Oh my Aideen, where are you now.
Sink like a stone, in a crowded room,
Oh my Aideen, where are you now.

Cold as a candle, I burned the night you left,
cold as a hanger in a gown,
cold as your blood, never more for to warm,
cold as a stone in the ground.

A crow flies over a neighboring hill,
Oh my Aideen, where are you now.
Another shot of whiskey, and take another pill,
Oh my Aideen, where are you now.

flowers, tintype

ode to apocalypse

Stirring, I grapple for sense in this wreck;
my drunken head deconstructed the globe?
I hear sirens wail through the fallen load,
and fled is that dream, thine strain inept.
Inept, incomplete, or insufficient?
Bid us all good sleep, within perfect tone,
because living is just to think and to groan?
What time have I to choose a soft blanket?
What tender night? What is joy without pain?
My agony pure; your music moot.
My breath still hot, and my frame now shaking,
Deathless Nightingale, cease! Your tune too crude;
beauty, raging, in redolent decay,
has no chance, for rapture is null and rude.

trunk and vine, tintype

the lone oak

As the clouds roll by,
I feel, so still.
As the moon shines through
I think of you, far away.

If we two should meet again,
in this barren land of broken gods,
where the wolves no longer hunt,
and lovers die alone,
if we two should meet again,
at the bare stump, where I stand,
we will not speak at once.

You will kiss my old forehead;
we will trust our blindness,
and eat the humble dust
that was peach
that was wine
that was love.

If we two should meet again
we will dream, together,
and our dreams will be host
for wayfarers and gods alike.

The mission of the wind will howl
through our entwined trunks,
but we will teach the wolves to hunt
and we will show them the belly
of a swollen moon.

We will become as one, here,
where the light surges and dims,

as the clouds pass by.
If we two should meet again,
we will not pronounce the other's name.

angst

out of the shower at 10 o'clock
and answering a phone call from the boss
"Shit," I say, "I overslept. Be right in."
"We start at 7, Lavoie.
I want to be done pruning, today."
"I know," I say,
"I'll be right in."

wanting some coffee, but the can is clean
lighting a smoke, and downing what is left in
the bottle of Riesling on the counter
then starting the car
and snaking down Roush Hill
to the river
and the vineyard.

forcing a corner
at 40 miles per hour
swerving to miss
a large something, in the road
running the passenger-side through a ditch
cutting the wheel hard
to get back out.

throwing open the car door
and shifting to my feet
witnessing the front tire
quickly going flat
scowling, but, plodding back,
to move the large something off the road

a snapping turtle.

reaching to seize him by his shell
his head and neck extending
further then I thought possible
pinching and severing
a bit of flesh from my
fingertip. "Motherfucker!"
jaws open and hissing at me.

bleeding and throbbing at the stubborn
fuck still possessing the road, but
finding a long stick and
pushing him, across the blacktop
rolling him, into the ditch.
watching him, watching me
through a cross, speckled eye.

jacking up the car
changing the flat tire
making it to work
as everyone else is taking lunch
no one saying, "Hi"
no one asking where I've been
while dressing my torn-open finger.

working late alone
to keep up with the schedule
pruning the vine
for fruiting, and for renewal
pruning the vine
diligently and
deliberately.

cleaning and honing my shears
oiling them and putting them up
sneaking coffee grounds
into a Ziplock bag
and two bottles
of chambourcin
into a five-gallon bucket.

returning at dusk
maneuvering passed
the many white churches
climbing Roush Hill
remembering the turtle
then, parking in the gravel
beside the rusting house trailer.

uncorking the wine
and cleaning a glass
for reading and suffering
these poems written
nights before; and feeling
somethings creeping about

a cockroach.

inching his way across
the yellowing kitchen floor
sensing
maybe
that he is being judged
and considering if
it is safer, under the stove.

flattening him
with my foot
hearing his body give
under the weight of me
pouring more wine
leaving the roach where he lies
crushed.

sitting drinking
the typewriter mocking me
the bookshelf, staring me down
Bukowski, shouting that I don't have the guts
Larry Brown, consenting that I'm just too nice
Carver, finishing a vodka
and looking entirely stoic

Wantling fighting off his demon
with a six pack and codeine
Hemingway
reminding me
it starts with one true sentence
and if I can't find that
I don't have the disease.

remembering my old man's dimly lit rented room
the smell of soiled laundry and cigarette smoke
finding him in the dark reading my notebook
approaching me intensely
pleading
"Please, don't write
any more of this shit."

one bottle gone, and uncorking another
noticing something going on
in the middle of the kitchen floor
ants, dismembering the dead roach I killed
watching
briefly
then killing the ants as well.

two bottles gone and
more ants needing killed
switching
to whiskey
their dead corpses growing in number
drinking and murdering
all night.

dozing, barely
in the wing chair
waking there
at five,
facing
the typewriter
understanding

there will be no rite
of passage but
ambling to the bath
in need of a shower
pushing the curtain aside, then
leaning into the tub and starting
the water.

"Jesus Christ!"

a spider

rapidly crawling out of the drain
propelling forward with
great eagerness
trying to escape the
rushing torrent.

trying to crawl up
the walls of the tub
thrilling, though
unsuccessful
but trying
again

trying

failing

trying

failing

stopping
maybe resting
maybe learning

…again.

remembering how
I'd been thinking her drowned
studying her
looking closely

seeing the shiny black body
and the red spot on her back
she's a widow

and it's unfortunate
I'll have to be killing her
for being true to the widow she is
but first
rising
walking to the kitchen
and making some coffee.

devil and his banjo, tintype

cello suite

the spotted fawn was struck
by a gold ford explorer
it flopped dead
in my driveway.
the girl in the ford wore hospital scrubs
cringed after hitting the deer
stopped briefly
and drove off.

i couldn't leave the little fawn
rotting twenty feet from my door
bringing in the buzzards
maggots
and flies.

i drug her by her hind legs
her head rambling
over the uneven earth
limp and lifeless.

i drug her deep
into the wooded hollow
and i stared back
at her blank stare.

later
in the house trailer
i washed my hands and fried a steak
drank a twelve pack of best
smoked
listened to Bach,
cello suites.

i could hear
the spotted fawn
wandering gaily

hopping in the tall grass
alongside the road
calling to me
just in time
to see the end.

the clock on the wall
was dumb.

the typewriter and
i too
was dumb.

i tried again, to
follow the deer, but
my words were stiff
i wasn't born to dance.

desperate to feel something
i drug the sledge out
from beneath the trailer.
i took it to the clock
then i went for the typewriter.

the first blow destroyed it,
but i kept on
blasting the thing to bits
until the end of the 2nd bourrée,
in suite no. 4.

i opened the last beer
and collapsed in the olive chair
the pieces were everywhere
i felt like
i might vomit
i couldn't go on.

i gathered the bent type bars
the keys and chards
of the carriage
to a box.
i took it to the woods
and placed it
beside the fawn.
the light was enough
to see the blank stare.
maybe it was
a triumphant death.

there wasn't anything to do
without the typewriter,
but it seemed best
to try to sleep.

skulls and bones, tintype

dead poem #9

C Dearest brother,
    Lion, like our will,
    august your fate,
    I've come to embrace
    you.

A How you fail to see the truth,
    even as it looks you
    in the eye?

    Alight at my forlorn side;
    recite to my bright ears,
    the chorus and verse
    of our years.

C Dearest brother,
    are we here just to sleep?
    Are we here
    just to dream?

A I know not more than you know.
    I've no conceit of forever;
    my kingdom's between
    the morning and
    evening.

C Then, should we believe
    that darkness
    forever
    bends about
    the light?"

A See that I shudder at
    the howling wind?
    It shakes my shadow thin,
    and causes the candles
    to tremble.

C Dearest brother,
    I will tend the fire.
    Take your rest.
    Take your rest.

A But I am anxious, too,
    as the wings about the flame.
    For melodious streams,
    my feeble ears do strain.
    Remind me some
    odes of ecstasy
    and ballads shaded
    by deep sorrow.
    Do not allow this hour
    go empty of song,
    should I not understand
    tomorrow.

the musician's fate, tintype

Jason Gerrish spent much of his formative years on the road, but at 27 slowed down and attempted to write a novel over a two-year sabbatical in a house trailer on Brad Daulton's farm. The poems in this collection first came about in that trailer, on Old State Road. Jason left the farm at 29, to attend Morehead State University, where he earned his BA and minored in creative writing. He writes to feel closer to the world and his experiences in it. Jason has been published in the Raw Art Review, where his poem "cello suite" was selected for the Charles Bukowski Prize for poetry.

Brad Daulton lives in Northside, Cincinnati, Ohio. He is a self-taught artist and musician. An advocate of creative self-expression, he is not tied to a single medium or form. The photographs published here, were taken at his family farm, in Manchester, Ohio. Brad's artwork has appeared in The Raw Art Review.

www.ingramcontent.com/pod-product-compliance
Lightning Source LLC
Chambersburg PA
CBHW041627220426
43663CB00004B/93